Bread Around the World

by Helen Gregory

Consultant:
Adria F. Klein, Ph.D.
California State University, San Bernardino

capstone classroom
Heinemann Raintree • Red Brick Learning
division of Capstone

People around the world eat bread.

Some bread is baked in a metal oven.

Some bread is baked in a clay oven.

Some bread is fried
in a pan.

Some bread is steamed in a basket.

Bread comes in many shapes and sizes.

Some bread is round.

Some bread is shaped like the moon.

Some bread has a hole in the middle.

Some bread is tied in a knot.

Some bread is flat
and crunchy.

Some bread is flat and soft.

This bread wraps around food.

This bread has a pocket.

Everyone eats bread!